Barcelona Travel Guide:

The Ultimate Barcelona, Spain Tourist Trip Travel Guide

By

Angela Pierce

Table of Contents

Introduction 5

Chapter 1. Climate 6

Chapter 2. Main Places to Visit 8

Chapter 3. Shopping.. 20

Chapter 4. Restaurants 21

Chapter 5. Nightlife - Clubs & Discos 27

Chapter 6. Additional Tips.. 29

Thank You Page 31

Barcelona Travel Guide: The Ultimate Barcelona, Spain Tourist Trip Travel Guide

By Angela Pierce

© Copyright 2015 Angela Pierce

Reproduction or translation of any part of this work beyond that permitted by section 107 or 108 of the 1976 United States Copyright Act without permission of the copyright owner is unlawful. Requests for permission or further information should be addressed to the author.

This publication is designed to provide accurate and authoritative information in regard to the subject matter covered. This work is sold with the understanding that the publisher is not engaged in rendering legal, accounting, or other professional services. If legal advice or other expert assistance is required, the services of a competent professional person should be sought.

First Published, 2015

Printed in the United States of America

Introduction

The minute you set your foot in Barcelona, you can't help but notice its pulsating energy which is as contagious as it is alluring. It is the capital of Catalonia region of Spain and definitely lives up to its reputation of a cosmopolitan city. This beach city has a modern vivacious vibe to it but at the same time it has held its traditions tight and undiluted. After all, not every city's tradition boasts of legends like Picasso, Joan Miro and Gaudi!

Barcelona has a thing or two for everyone who comes to this city. There are golden beaches lapping up with azure blue waters, historical gems and architectural marvels, a never-ending nightlife and food that makes you go weak in the knees! Whatever be your area of interests, you can pack your nights and days with Barcelona and yet you would not have had enough of this effervescent city

Chapter 1. Climate

Hot, Cold and Thunderstorms

Barcelona has a sub-tropical climate where winters never get too cold and the highest temperature usually never soars beyond 30 degrees Celsius. This actually makes Barcelona a great getaway year round. Typically the seasons here are categorized as follows:

- Winter: November to February

-Spring: March to May

-Summer: June to August

-Autumn: September to October

From tourist's point of view, it is better to concentrate on months and their average temperatures and not the season. If you are planning for a lot of outdoor action then months between November to April seem ideal. The temperature in this period hovers between thirteen to seventeen degrees during days. However you can expect overcast sky and slight rain during this season. Nights in December and January do get cold but the temperatures are not near freezing. You can venture out in warm woolen clothing.

Famous beaches of Barcelona are best enjoyed during warmer season from May to July and September to October. August is generally the hottest month here in Barcelona and humidity can worsen it. But for rest of the summer time, humidity remains quite low and there is hardly any rain. Persistent sea breeze makes for a very pleasant weather even at high temperature.

However, of the entire Spain, Barcelona has the least predictable weather owing to its geographical location along Costa Brava. So, there are times when you might be met with an overcast sky which refuses to subside even after 3-4 days!

Chapter 2. Main Places to Visit

Barcelona boasts of some of the best museums in the world. The architectural splendors are strewn across Barcelona rightfully boasting of being home to the legendary architect Gaudi. This picturesque city has a celebratory undercurrent to it and the best place to experience this is the scenic beaches with Barcelona's skyline in the backdrop. If you are travelling with kids, then Barcelona makes for a great choice. Amusement parks, world class aquariums and chocolate factory are sure to catch their attention. Here we present the list of "must-see" attractions when in Barcelona.

Museu Picasso

Pablo Picasso is amongst the most extraordinary artistes in the world history. A very few like him came and fewer still made their mark. Barcelona is Picasso's city where he completed his apprenticeship as an artist and he himself chose Barcelona for a museum dedicated to his Artwork. Therefore a visit to this city without making it to this museum is incomplete in its spirit. This museum was opened to public in 1963 and is located at number 15 Carrer De Montcada. The museum also houses Sabartés's personal collection and showcases 39 artworks in total. The 13th-15th century buildings where this museum is, are actually palaces created in Catalan civic gothic style- artwork in themselves!

Barceloneta Beach

More than a kilometer of golden sand and gushing waves welcome you to the most famous beach of Barcelona. It is believed to be the setting for the fight between Don Quixote and Knight of the White moon! This beach has complete amenities for those who want to spend a relaxing day here. Functional public toilets, showers, life guards, changing rooms, beach umbrellas, loungers and restaurants make this beach one of the most comfortable and tourist friendly. If you are the sporty kind, then indulge in some beach volleyball, tennis, wind surfing, Kite surfing or just take a dip and go for a swim. This beach also flaunts popular but bizarre "Homenatge a la Barceloneta"- a structure that looks like a modern day building but leaning on one side.

Casa Batlló

This building screams of Antoni Gaudi's style and why not, he is the one to put it on Barcelona's map! The unmissable colourful facade of the building is done with pieces pf mosaic and the texture of roof bears a strong semblance to the skin of a dragon. The building was built by Gaudi and later renovated on the request of Batlló family who wanted a unique and never seen before home for them. Today this building is open to public and many artistic events take place here. Another remarkable feature of this building is almost a complete absence of straight lines!

Sagrada Família

Yet another landmark of Barcelona from the master creator Gaudi, it is an incomplete basilica. The actual construction of this building was started in 1882 but came to a standstill in 1926 when Gaudi passed away unexpectedly. Since then there have been various attempts to complete the structure but nothing seems to give justice to this creation of Gaudi. Right from the use of material to design sensibilities, the construction has always been in the eye of storm. Make it early in the day to Sagrada Família since entry is restricted to a particular number citing safety issues and the queue is understandably long. You can also book the tickets online and give a miss to queue altogether!

Plaça de Catalunya

This is Barcelona's answer to Times Square but with a difference that Plaça de Catalunya boasts of architectural treasures from the likes of Gaudi! It is a huge area and features many famous artworks in form of sculptures. The most popular amongst them are Monument of Francesc Macià and statue of La Deessa created by Josep Clara. This place is amongst the busiest landmarks of the city as nine streets open up. There are numerous oval benches placed here where you can sit and watch the crowds pass by. Fountains and landscaping around the square makes it an extremely pleasant place to catch your breath at!

Barcelona Cathedral

This cathedral is seat of the Archbishop of Barcelona and flaunts gothic style architecture. The cathedral is a work of Art with magnificent altar pieces painted by Guerau Gener, Lluís Borrassà, Gabriel Alemany and

Bernat Martorell. Barcelona Cathedral includes alabaster tomb of Santa Eulalia, one of Barcelona's Patron saints who was killed by Romans. The choir here occupies Central position and the Organ is located to the side which is a huge departure from the usual plan of other European churches. If you want to enter this spectacular building then dress conservatively conforming to the rules of a place of worship. Permission to entry can be denied if what you wear irks the watchman!

Marbella Beach

How can we stay away from beaches when in Barcelona! Marbella is another popular beach for those who want to get that beautiful Spanish tan, laze around on the warm sand and cool heels in the lovely blue waters. This nudist beach is also a haven for water sports enthusiasts. Windsurfing, kayaking and sailing trips here are quite popular. This beach also has a diving centre, racing track, skate-park and a full-fledged sports complex. Just like other beaches in Barcelona, Marbella also has amenities like showers, changing rooms, Wi-Fi, life guards, restaurants and public toilets. For kids, this beach has some shielded portion where they can play in the safe calm waters.

MACBA Barcelona Art Museum

MACBA art museum exhibits contemporary art belonging to the late 20th century. An important aspect of this museum is that the art work is exhibited temporarily and changes every three to six months. This place has featured many international artistes like Fontana, Saura and Klee. The exhibits here range from sculptures to films along with various workshops that are held here from time to time. This museum was thrown open to public in 1995 and the museum building was designed by Richard Meier which exudes contemporary sensibilities. Check on the current shows and workshops if you are planning to make a stop here.

Magic Fountain (Font Magica)

This fountain in Avinguda Maria Cristina has been mesmerizing crowds since 1929. It was designed by Charles Buigas for Great universal exhibition and about 3000 men worked to build this marvellous play of jet streams, music and light. The light and sound show of

Magic fountain takes place in the evenings and lasts over an hour. The jet stream of water changes colour and its movement is coordinated with music. Magic fountain is not one but conglomeration of multiple fountains that throw up about thirty water arrangements that create magic that steals your heart and thus the name!

Parc De La Ciutadella

Ciutadella Park was originally created for 1888 Universal exhibition by architect Josep Fontseré. The garden houses stunning Castell dels Tres Dragons, a cascading waterfall and a lake where you can rent a boat. The vast expanse of 18 hectares and lush greenery of this park has made it famous as "green lungs of Barcelona". The Barcelona zoo stands at one end of this park making it a very ideal place for children. Replica of the famous sculpture "El desconsol" by Josep Llimona also sits pretty in this park. Catalan parliament building is also located on one side of Ciutadella.

Jardi Botanic

This botanical garden gives you a glimpse of fauna from Australia, Chile, South Africa, California, Canary Island and three Mediterranean zones. You can come across some rare species of plants around the world right here in this garden. There are pretty paths, small water bodies and information on all plants is sufficiently given on the boards. It is quite a walk that can last over forty five minutes. Spread over 14 hectares, this stunning garden gives a breath-taking view of Barcelona, Freight port and Olympic sports venue. Due to the height at which this garden is located, it may pose some challenges for old and really young children. But the hike is worth the view and collection here!

Parc Güell

Parc Güell gives a spectacular view of the city and the park itself is a work of art. This park was designed by Gaudi and so there is an unmistakable "Gaudi Aura" here. This park was Güell's vision of British residential park which was executed by Gaudi. The most striking feature of the park includes Dragon stairway with twin flight of stairway rising from the entrance. The grandeur of this park is accentuated by the Hypostyle room and a Greek style open theatre which is now known as the Nature square. This stunning estate also features Austria garden, named so because the trees here were donated by Austria in 1977.

L'Aquarium de Barcelona

If you are accompanied by kids, then this is one attraction you can't miss. This aquarium is the largest in Mediterranean region and has fish and aquatic species from all around the world. There are about 35 tanks with 11,000 animals. What makes this place lot more exciting is an eighty meter long underwater tunnel, one and only in entire Europe! Not exciting enough for you? Try diving in the shark tank!

Maritime Museum

Maritime museum showcases the maritime heritage and history of this port city. Located in the old town, this museum has been built inside former shipyards. The museum covers maritime history of Barcelona starting from 1400's into the present times. There are ships as exhibits here including a three mast merchant vessel 'Santa Eulàlia' and a full sized model of a Royal barge. Apart from these, a wooden submarine, fishing vessel and racing boats can be seen here. There is an impressive collection of old navigational tools and other exhibits that belong to Catalan ships of 19th century. Visit this museum to pamper the seafaring adventurer in you!

Catalan National Art Museum

The majestic building that houses National Art museum was originally built for World fair of 1929. This building was refurbished and opened to public in 1990 as the museum that stands today. This museum features world's largest collection of Roman frescoes that were rescued from 29 churches before being destroyed in Spanish civil war. With 260,000 artworks exhibited here, Catalan National Art Museum is the most important and largest museum of Barcelona. You can witness Catalan art collection belonging to period between 19th and early 20th century. There are also exhibits from renaissance and a collection of 130,000 coins here. If you are an avid art lover then reserve at least half a day for this very informative and attractive museum.

Casa Mila

One more of architectural genius of Gaudi, designing of Casa Mila was assigned to him by Pedro Milà i Camps after he saw Casa Batllo. This building bears the signature style of Gaudi by being unconventional and breaking the accepted norms of architecture. The interior of the building lacks straight lines and is a mix of expressionist and Nouveau style. The top floors and roof terrace with its unusual chimneys are open to public. It is also the largest civil structure made by Gaudi. There are audio guided tours here and an elevator is available to take the patrons up. However, while coming down one has to use the staircases only.

Museu de la Xocolata

This museum is chocolate lover's paradise and an absolutely delightful experience for children. The museum covers history of chocolate in Europe and its manufacturing from cocoa beans to a finished sumptuous delicacy! To the amusement of visitors, a piece of chocolate is given to everyone who enters the museum. Even adults can learn a thing or two as they absorb information on chocolate. Did you know chocolate was considered divine in some ancient cultures? This and many other facts get a voice here. Do not forget to pick some home-made chocolates from the shop here as you finish the tour of the museum.

Parc d'Atraccions Tibidabo

Give an adrenaline rush to the adventure seeker in you with 360 degree turns and sudden plunges that make your heart beat like it is going to pop out! This century old park features vintage rides of the foregone era along with high tech ones that are very today. World's first flight simulator, haunted castle, Talaia belonging to year 1921, 50 metres high Ferris wheel are some of the exciting rides you can enjoy here. The location of the park is also fantastic which is on the top of a hill giving you a stunning view of the city and beachfront. Two elevators service the park and make it convenient to reach the hilltop especially with children.

Chapter 3. Shopping

La Rambla

La Rambla is a stretch of 1.2 kilometres that joins Christopher Columbus monument to the City Centre. If you fancy a leisurely walk along a boulevard of trees while soaking up on the sounds and smell of this lovely city then La Rambla is the place to be. For those who want to indulge in street shopping, La Rambla does present a decent option. For avid serious shopaholics, this place is heaven! There are many known restaurants and street shops located here. But a word of caution- beware of pickpockets!

Shopping Malls

If you are looking for shopping malls where you would like to spend more time on shopping then you should visit Diagonal Mar, L'illa Diagonal, Pedralbes Centre, Maremagnum and Centro Comercial Glòries shopping malls.

Chapter 4. Restaurants

After a whole lot of sight- seeing and roaming around the scenic city of Barcelona, it is time to catch up on some food. We would not be exaggerating if we call Barcelona a gastronomical paradise. This city pampers the foodie in you and tingle your taste buds with flavours that scintillate and aroma that allures. The food culture of the city is worth exploring and if you have time on hand then dedicate a few days doing just that!

Dos Palillos Restaurant

This Michelin starred restaurant has been opened by Chef Albert Raurich and its speciality is Asian cuisine served in typical Tapas style! The experimental food is not the only attraction but also the pleasure of watching chefs working like expert craftsman on your food is an absolutely mouth- watering experience. Dos Palilios brings best of the Asian food particularly Japanese and gives it a Spanish soul!

Moments

Here is another two starred Michelin restaurant that reflects elegance and sophistication of fine dining and is part of Hotel Mandarin Oriental. This restaurant features tasting menu with Spanish and Asian dishes and an excellent wine list. The food here is known for its creativity and they go an extra mile to pair the delicacies being served with the right wine!

Arola Restaurant

Dig into some crafty Mediterranean food and delectable tapas here at Arola. Belonging to master chef Sergi Arola, the menu here includes 6 course prefix tapas and the tapas look like pieces of art; after all its Barcelona- a city that breathes art! The restaurant offers magnificent view of the city and DJ who plays the music that goes along the ambience of this restaurant.

Passadis Del pep

Barcelona boasts of freshest sea catch in the Mediteranean and so it hardly comes as a surprise that this city has innumerable restaurants serving sea food.

However, Passadis Del pep stands out in the crowd with its family style serving in a cozy ambience and absolutely gorgeous food! This restaurant is a must for intense foodie. There is no menu and whatever is cooked is served to you which feels like a surprise fest as well.

Can Valles Restaurant

Do not be fooled by its humble appearance, Can valles can easily give the biggest restaurants in barcelona a run for their money. It is a great value for money restaurant that serves Tapas, salads, grilled delicacies and desserts that ooze refinement and impress with their impeccable presentation.

Petit Comite

Located in the city's gastronomy alley at Passatge de la concepcio 13 Petit Comite is owned by Chef Nandu Jubany. It is famous for its seasonal menu and the restaurant itself is a great place to host your own small get together. The seasoned chef here can customise the menu according to your tastes and desire. The dishes are slow cooked and made with the best produce available. An extensive menu features Tapas, appetizers, starters and loads of mains!

Tickets

Owned by renowned chefs who are also brothers- Albert and Ferran Adria. Tickets is not only a popular restaurant but also a busy bar. If you want to eat at this restaurant then advance bookings are recommended as the restaurant is usually fully booked for months. The feel of the restaurant is very informal and the menu is amusingly colourful and quirky! While there, do try their famous "elBulli olives" and be ready to be surprised!

A Sip & a swig – Bars

Let your spirits go high and get tipsy over a few drinks and great conversations while you are here in Barcelona. The cosmopolitan vibe of this city can be seen and experienced in its full glory at the awesome bars and cafés that spring at every turn here. Here is the pick of most popular and recommended bars that define the 'high' culture of Barcelona!

Speak Easy Dry Martini'

This is believed to be the oldest bar here in the city and boy does it feel like stepping into the bygone era! They serve one of the best cocktails in the city and staff is super friendly. Unique ambience definitely scores extra brownie points here.

Ginger

You may have a little difficulty finding this one but ones you find it, you would probably end up here every evening! Ginger is not only popular for its extravagant cocktail menu but also mouth-watering tapas that they serve here.

Boca Grande

This bar has the most glamourous interiors in all of Barcelona. The open roof top cocktail bar only adds to the already awesome ambience here. Try their menu of sea food along with drinks.

Electric Bar

Electric bar is popular amongst the younger crowd owing to their live gigs and performances. A great place to jam over a few drinks. What more, this bar is definitely high on value for money quotient.

Kasparo

Kasparo gives a glimpse of city's culture as it is quite popular amongst the locals here. It has a quiet cosy ambience and a delectable menu to go with drinks. It is highly recommended for those who have children along as this bar situated right opposite a small park!

Torre Rosa

This bar is housed in an old barcelona style bunglow with a garden terrace which has a gorgeous ambience owing to the tree line that surrounds it. It has a very pretty setting and serves only drinks, no food.

Shams Lounge

This bar has dim lighting, comfortable and cosy seating along with a very relaxed ambience. Buddha statues, bamboo tables and a mix of medditeranean and Asian sensibilities make Shams lounge a great place to have a few drinks and catching up on life in general.

Chapter 5. Nightlife - Clubs & Discos

Barcelona has an impressive and wild nightlife. The clubs here almost never close and parties go on till wee hours of the morning. Best music from around the world and heart thumping beats keep the party travelers going strong all night!

One of the most popular discotheques here is **The Warehouse BCN** which is an underground club famous for its music and happening crowd. **Razzmatazz** takes clubbing to an entirely different league. It has five clubs under one roof and is located in downtown Barcelona. Experience the sounds of indie rock, techno and pop here with each club hosting its own theme! Another popular haunt of Catalans and tourists alike is **Luz De Gas** which has been built in an old music hall theatre. The live music here is very popular and the setting is definitely classy and sophisticated.

When it comes to partying, no one does better than **The Sutton Club.** They are known for featuring the best DJ's around the world and holding exclusive parties that go from completely entertaining to completely wild! Apart from parties, they also host events and invite best of music talent on their floors.

Chapter 6. Additional Tips

Barcelona inspires and surprises those who choose to revel in the colours of this fabulous city. Plan a trip but make sure it is not rushed because there is so much to see and experience here that you will always be left with some place unseen and unexplored. Food should be on the highest pedestal on your bucket list if you are planning a trip to this part of the world. I would recommend a detailed planning and advanced bookings if gastronomical tourism is your priority here.

As far as the accommodation is concerned, you have various options ranging from budget to star hotels. But along with deciding on the budget, it would be imperative to determine the area of your stay as well. Say, whether you would want to soak up the gorgeous beach view or rich hill side. Staying in the city centre has its own advantages but of course it comes with the disadvantage of being amidst the noisy city crowd.

The public transport system, particularly Metro is a great way of getting across the city. Taxi service is also available however it is a bit pricey. An extensive network of Public transport system exists in the City which includes buses, metros and trams. There is an integrated ticket system prevalent here. Passes make it further inexpensive to travel in the public transport. There are six zones and therefore six types of tickets. Zone I covers most of the city and airport whereas rest of all cover the outskirts and far off areas.

So make a plan and visit this wonderful city which is as exciting as that football team which is named after this great city!

Thank You Page

I want to personally thank you for reading my book. I hope you found information in this book useful and I would be very grateful if you could leave your honest review about this book. I certainly want to thank you in advance for doing this.

If you have the time, you can check my other books too.

www.ingramcontent.com/pod-product-compliance
Lightning Source LLC
LaVergne TN
LVHW021746060526
838200LV00052B/3501